THE KINDNESS COLDER
THAN THE ELEMENTS

MINGLING VOICES
Series editor: Manijeh Mannani

Give us wholeness, for we are broken.
But who are we asking, and why do we ask?
— PHYLLIS WEBB

National in scope, Mingling Voices draws on the work
of both new and established poets, novelists, and writers
of short stories. The series especially, but not exclusively,
aims to promote authors who challenge traditions and
cultural stereotypes. It is designed to reach a wide variety
of readers, both generalists and specialists. Mingling
Voices is also open to literary works that delineate the
immigrant experience in Canada.

SERIES TITLES

Poems for a Small Park
  E.D. Blodgett

Dreamwork
  Jonathan Locke Hart

Windfall Apples: Tanka and Kyoka
  Richard Stevenson

The dust of just beginning
  Don Kerr

Roy & Me: This Is Not a Memoir
  Maurice Yacowar

Zeus and the Giant Iced Tea
  Leopold McGinnis

Praha
  E.D. Blodgett

Musing
  Jonathan Locke Hart

Dustship Glory
  Andreas Schroeder

The Kindness Colder Than the Elements
  Charles Noble

poems

CHARLES NOBLE

The Kindness Colder
Than the Elements

AU PRESS

Copyright © 2011 Charles Noble
Published by AU Press, Athabasca University
1200, 10011 – 109 Street, Edmonton, AB T5J 3S6

ISBN 978-1-926836-24-9 (print)
ISBN 978-1-926836-25-6 (PDF)
ISBN 978-1-926836-64-5 (epub)

A volume in the Mingling Voices series:
ISSN 1917-9405 (print)   1917-9413 (digital)

Cover and interior design by Natalie Olsen, Kisscut Design
Printed and bound in Canada by Marquis Book Printers.

LIBRARY AND ARCHIVES CANADA CATALOGUING IN PUBLICATION
Noble, Charles, 1945–
The kindness colder than the elements / Charles Noble.

(Mingling voices)
Poems.
Issued also in electronic formats.
ISBN 978-1-926836-24-9

I. Title. II. Series: Mingling voices
PS8577.O32K56 2011   c811'.54   C2011-905130-3

We acknowledge the financial support of the Government
of Canada through the Canada Book Fund (CBF) for our
publishing activities.

Canada Council   Conseil des Arts
for the Arts   du Canada

To the memory of Robert Kroetsch,
who knew how to hang in uncertainty, but who,
in another opposite than from this Keatsian negative,
was so positive.

ACKNOWLEDGEMENTS

I would like to thank Walter Hildebrandt for his ongoing exchange of ideas and his encouragement. And Pamela MacFarland Holway for her exquisite and intelligent editorial eye. I thank Natalie Olsen for her book design — her careful reading and keen sense for the right cover art. I thank Megan Hall for coordinating the various ports that myself and the others here are and for then steering the book into open waters.

I would once again like to thank Marlene Lacey for her advice and troubleshooting re my unruly computer while the manuscript was in preparation. Finally, I would like to thank the two external readers engaged by AU Press for obviously taking the writing seriously and for their insightful comments.

... the thin alternatives of a utilitarianism
of wants or a contractualism of rights.
In this reduction, any active conception
of citizenship vanishes. We are left with
the roles of mere consumers or litigants.

PERRY ANDERSON, *The New Old World* (p. 120)

::

... the dominant imperative in the world
today is "Live without an Idea."

ALAIN BADIOU, *The Communist Hypothesis* (p. 231)

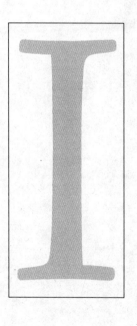

...whereas it is the harshest and most glaring of contradictions when the form determinations of the syllogism, which are Notions, are treated as notionless material.

G.W.F. HEGEL, *Science of Logic*
(Humanities Paperback Library edition, p. 684)

...the logical proposition or syllogism — suddenly proves to be the very vehicle for Life itself and the beating heart of the Notion or Begriff, the final stage of the Hegelian thought process. (Hegel's revival and transmogrification of the millennially mummified scholastic version of Aristotle's logic, his transformation of these dead forms back into genuine philosophical conceptuality, was of course his most intellectually original and audacious philosophical act.)

FREDRIC JAMESON, *The Hegel Variations* (p. 39)

Cars are big zoomers
My car only goes 140
Therefore I get out and take a look
At the thing turn around
Digest its own overhead

Just like the *Herald*
Up a head
Till the boats all rise.

⁜

The future is a sell-out
The way we think now

A vacuum of sorts
Into which mean things
Will rush

Take my sins
Some will go straight up
In smoke

Some will coincide
With this future
As omission

Therefore the only solution
Is a set of super omissions

The under-men
In remissionary positions

These castrations
Already cheating
My simple intentions.

⁂

The *pièce de résistance*
Is around the corner
I mean over the hill, weak
And agèd that is

Therefore my dessert
Wants its extra
s sent back to the kitchen.

⁑

Cars are big zoomers
My car likes the garage

The garage doesn't like
The house
Us boys like the garage too
All the implements in the end

But mostly because the castle
Has so much to lose

We sit on the cheap nylon lawn chairs
And smell the Martian tires

Just as Detroit there
In its cockade and cackle
Asks the cooper
So skeuomorphic
So adjective above
For a hoopless barrel.

⁙

The Blues are a much-loved genre
I pitched my tent
In centre field

Therefore a pre-autographed ball
Slipped out

Rolled over
And followed up the foul line

To the fence
Where the used-to-be-lime
Has drawn the line.

::

Costs are astronomical
I have the Keynes
To the Kingdom

Therefore I'm not kidding
When I say
This seat is reserved

Come back younger
Than your twin
And it'll still be
Reserved

(Ernest Mandel says
K's *"Après-nous-le-Déluge"*-expansive-
But-cutting-it-short
"In the long run we're all dead"
Gives it away).

∷

The sun is not cold
So I lose the gloves
But my hands start to ache

Some kids
Would have no feelings
One way or another
About this ache
If they had it
And they usually do

Therefore the centipede crashes
But the gold bug vacuums up.

⁘

The South Sea Bubble
Or speculative genome
As we know it
Divines the genome
The cars traffic the stars
Or tether way around

Therefore "monkeys for sale,
If you're the type."

⠿

I am not the king
Who dots the rational state's *i*

It could be The Bay, an airport
Or Isaac Asimov in Eaton's
Or simply the not simple
Noise from nowhere

Therefore I am
The big little *I*
Touching my toes in the bathroom
In the cheer leaders' wind

The out there procreation bowl
Touches down

It's full or was
Of we pee peewees.

⁛

All the aches in their loins
Don't add up
So my heart
Aches for them

Just as you were grooving
On the tongue's
Perfectly empty
Cow cups

Therefore "l love you"
Is as good
As having a team
To root for

Sweat quantums up
To sweater
Therefore the spirit
Of the place
Gets traded
In the long draft
Between sips.

::

Elmer Fudd hat
Big moose gun
Pretty fucking obvious

Therefore Hitler
Into the shredder

Soup's on
I mean
Soupçon

Not so obvious
In fact, oysters aside
Down right
You-only-think-of-it-
Later

Timeless
In the original sense of
Shirtless, say.

∷

My shoulders have left most of their cartilage
In the gym and some granaries

Therefore body-building now
Becomes a few bricks
Short of a load

Each creak
Of the joints
I step into the new

Let's face it
I get old
But not the old hat.

::

Things are closing in on me
I'm not going mad
I'm just in a crowded bar

Therefore why am I here
Said the comedian
Forgetting his pathetic path

The point being
You can turn it all
Back on itself

Then pocket
The rest.

::

He called me *dude*
"Sorry dude"
As he accidentally bumped me

The list goes on
And I'm a little listless

Therefore, knowing this
Dude business
I've not been "bumped"

As I was out of line
Already

Rather I've been raised
By the kids

By the modernist's "sub-mass"
Just as the elite goes out.

⁑

The Fido movie
Fetching fidelity
In the service trucks
Outside of circulation
But positing it
With lipstick as we say now
Long after Job's daughter
Eye Shadow

Dog wags
The absolute detail
And thereby hangs

For that matter
Any number of dogs
Would have done

Albeit movie takes
This particular life

Therefore tears are sweet
I mean wheat
Swept up

Homesick runs away
So to foundling itself
Up in the air
Who care

The dog sicks
To death

Flies on an orange peel
Flies in the face
Fighting back the rainbow thing.

∷

Stopped in my tracks
I have a fish in my shoe
Therefore: surrealism

Within the horizon
Of evolution
We add quickly

Slowly we go
Nevertheless
Speed is involved

Therefore: therefore
Tip of the top up
Hats on the way
Off

The fancy night bouncing
On a bed of Coleridge

The mistless Canadarm
Feather of the man
In-vents the air
Right out his hair.

⁘

Farmers here are neither peasants
Nor aristocrats
In some futurism
They are the living dead
Going around and around
We kid each other
From our tractors

We are the salt in our wounds
How do you like that
Seed in the ground

But of course
We listen to the talk shows

Therefore we know
We scratch
The little earth
From the satellites
Like all the other bred and better hens.

::

South on Highway 2
First light
Traffic accident

Fire trucks, police cars
Crunched-up cars

Infinitely adjusted
A car seat
Recalls the factory
A worker makes theatre
Sitting on a joke

But us the flow
Detour right
Whip back, turn right
And continue
The flow

Therefore flow
Is given head

Therefore the flow
Is given its head

Which means
Scottish roundabouts
Or traffic circles
Are rare here

Except the accident
The compressed cars
Squeeze out the intact
Humans
Totalled plus

I'm Mr. Electrons
Shorting with the radio referents
Otherwise off to Mars
Utensilling through the kitchen

Except out of the humans
Is squeezed something else

The final caurse
The jars of life
Teetering off and on the shelf

Flow's points deciding either
Say West
Or departure.

::

Take basketball
Great catch and release
Ball of the little other

Or better nyet
Take (Russian) hockey

Ya gotta have a team
A jersey
"Rooting for laundry"

You have no roots
In a neutral equilibrium
But the underdog flicks you on
Where you always lose even
If not

Not because you must prop or propel
The underdog
But your rooting is rootless
Even as homo sapiens as such are
Which is why they grow them
Retroactively
A sum or a summer
Or a Sumerian story

Tell this story to a cognitive interruption
And the two of them between them
Create the laundry

Dirty laundry
Whose roots you clean
Above futility and utility
At both ends burning.

::

I haven't
much time

I might add
This morning

Therefore
The gorge
Is stuffed

I'm running
Out of Crete

Island of better halves
Espousals of women
Just like men
With a period

A term
Come to term.

⁂

Someone's in the alley
With Dinah
I mean the diners
Across the alley
Produce garbage
One way or another
The kitchen staff
Dumps into the bin

The garbage trucks
Will be along
With futile equations
Charismatic Arendtian futility
Producing not a square meal
But a circle
Therefore square one

One who while dying
Gets out of bed
To bow
To the figure
Entered and re-entered.

::

One thing
Lead to gold
Well of course
I kid

One thing to another
Series world
Baseball say

I met Mickey Mantle
Or his mantle
Or a Canadian connection
In a series of loose pucks

Therefore all
Is dispirited

Without teeth
With various spirits

All games lost
It's not even
Winnie-the-Pooh

The blue lines
Have left the building

A year's supply
Of your own shit
Will power a light bulb
For ten hours

The house is tired
Of putting out winnings.

::

I did my duty
Made you a star

The moonshine
You subsisted on
Vapourized the moon
Let the shine
Shine on

Therefore I can
Relax now
Let your mucky muck personality
Return to muck
Where I too
Treat my curious spark
To the carious cure

Rooms for improvement
Can't decide
Whether to trim the hedge
Or bet the farm.

∷

How right
She said of the torn-out décor

Write something pretty
She said

Therefore the pink snake
On the rosy hardwood

Securitized debt hardwired
Nest to the baby bird rictus
Of the porn star.

∷

Garbage trucks arrive
In the predawn

In an ideal world
They scoop me up
Flip me over
And truck-tuck me away

Therefore in a countermove
To the noise befalling
My ideal sleep situation
Eats god knows what
Before the serial cereal

Sees that it is good
These very accurate clunks in the dark

The long arm of the alarm
Complete with voices skipping the beat

Chaplins of industry
Coming out

Of their own
Their fellow travelling
Dead labour.

::

We stand on giants
Well some of us
On Labradors

Do Labradors
Dogs that is
Exist?

Air brakes
Break wind
From time to time
Air to air

It's not earth to
Hey words

To err
Is human
All too human
As the evil anvil hammer tweeted

Therefore get out
Over the overtaken waters
Smell the deflowered moon

The twist of untwisted ankles
Where the gravity let up.

::

The awful recorded drumming coming
Through
Is a leisure pursuit

It is the expression
Of something not
Getting it right

The philosophy of industry
Service or otherwise
Is bent out of shape

I eat the restaurant meal
With a smile
And secondary exchanges
In the falsetto range
Therefore we all pay twice
Once on time

Once at our leisure.

::

The first one
Is trying to dissolve
Your agitated knowledge
Carnal all-know
Nothing

The other one
Also a woman
Is trying to put the genie
Back in
The smoothed out
Innocent skin
Formerly known as
Folded infinity
In a box

Yes the jocular
Vulgar box
Cum vox

Saying
Out of the blue face

There's a hole in your head
Why don't I pop in?

∷

"Life is too short"
He said
A hobby aesthete
Shooting from the hip

As the reason not to read
Difficult books

Another decade
Goes by
And the spaghetti sauce
Curls up on his cheeks
A clown's mouth

His belly arrives
Everywhere first
Shorting the long labour
That awaits some signal

That close to the bone
Solves anything

Therefore that guy
With neuralgia
Who provides
So many academics
With chew

Spoke always
Of his labours
Mental labours
Not *corvée*

Under the sop to Cerberus
The calculating brain calculated his death

His labour
Went over the moon
Just like the moron cow

His milk was the kindness
Higher but colder than the elements.

::

The psyche, say
And its pretensions
Are bound
To run
Into the hot stove
League
Get hurt

Regardless of how
These pretensions
Cut into
The truth or not

Therefore it
The adventitious ego, say
Becomes a cloud

The root undoing the seed
And the emergent plant
Undoing the seed

Find themselves
If they do
Undeceived

And they do
Reined in
Under the outed cloud.

∷

Now the not so big gelding
Was in love with the mare
We liked to sentimentalize

At any rate
The mare was the boss
Or bitch we like to camp up on

In the cold wind-chilled
December day
Not long from sunset
I drove into the yard
And the gelding heard me first
Came galloping down the lane
As I approached
The timothy and alfalfa bales

He slammed on the brakes
Turned tail
And was out of sight
Like I'd scared him

Then I said
"I better go tell Nickie"
To the virtual stirrup

A nice thought therefore
I've synthesized love and fear
Down meaning down
On the farm
Under the hay
Warming up
For the hoof
Compounded by the opalescent farrier

At the edge of the forest
Where the dissembling trees assemble.

::

He's taken to judging
What he judges stupidity

But won't exactly
Pin the tail

Others he meets
Make perfect donkeys
He would judge
Except for the zoo
He keeps natural

He turns a turned tail
To endless instrument

Which we always admit
Measures our progress
Into morass

The instrument
Like capital takes flight

And like capital
Kneads the morass
But doesn't seem
To know it.

::

My ailments come and go
Talking of the Michael's chain store
Their framing department

The bold shoulders
And alimentary canals
Of the rugby boys
We know
Have a long après ski

But it's true
The breath knocked out
Was there all the time

Till now
The temporary recall.

∷

Lots of broccoli
And counting

Capital set up my computer
So it writes "Betty [Who-shall-remain ...]"
An old schoolmate
Who wrote me an email

Betty might not like
This better mouse trap

Therefore I betchya Betty
This between the lines divinity
Or boson buzz
Does

Yet deism insists
So then Agatha clicks.

⁘

Everything I express
Comes back
As you
Phony as all get out

Except you switch things
Up on me
With a foundering boat

Therefore I take it apart
Plank by plank
Gang plank what's left
Fuck all.

::

I like getting mad
At people

Use it as a kind
Of sleeping pill

So nice to night night
The nightie of the anti-Turin machine
The nightmare neighing

It's all right
To have enemies

For
The cause

Therefore when I get up
To pee good heart
I have to admit
I'm pissed off

Pillow of thistles
I'm that other
Mad
Wrestler

Ground down till
The morning

Turns up
Tiller the Thriller.

::

Birds fly by
The window
Don't ask

What kind of birds
Birds don't exist

You say
Politically incorrect

And I say not
That I'm actually
Sticking up for birds
Their due

I'm simply stating
The facts

Therefore Marilyn Monroe
In Banff
Hit the papers

Robert Mitchum
Went down the Bow River
Where it drops to its knees

Shit load
Of Niagara false.

\:\:

The ex-con declared
He was a human being
Had spirituality

I say
I'm not proud
As a reflex
More than I say
I'm proud
Of my bones

Therefore
A bit of anti-tulip service
To get the Netherlands
Up to sea level
To some sum
See you one.

::

He prepared the deposits
Destined for the recycling bins
Two trips down
To the room
Smelly
Though the big doors open
Daily for the trucks

Cardboard into cardboard
Bin

Regular garbage into another
Compost into the smelliest

Rinsed-out milk and cream
Cartons into plastic shuttle

Plastic into a rubber
Or indeed plastic or hybrid barrel

Wine bottles
Into a compartmentalized box

A heavy stack of newspapers
Plopped into barrel
Close to full

Of among things
A murder of receipts
That flutter up
And float away
Like blossoms
With the *merde* to power

Therefore on the way out
He pauses inspired
With his hand on the door handle

Farts and rolls around
There is
No last of it.

∷

Again I consider
The lout oh corn
I don't know
The term

Bastard off the mark
Villain lite
In real life
Heavy enough

But caught
In a vulnerable act
Tied into eating
What they saw him
Coming for
And served

He structurally estranged
And a bit drunk
Took back the alien

Condescendingly inspected
His neighbour
With prejudice
And inward but a bit outward
Histrionics
That spilled back
Into his drink

Thus sobered
And cum the cricket
Talking to himself
From the counter top
Of the bar's bar

Therefore I throw him
A drone

Before he gives me
A kiss.

::

Other than legs
What did the Romans
Have?

Other than the Greeks
To kick around
Knickknacks of,
What?

Could the subject
Be too big for me?

Therefore I'm just
A gibbon
For Gibbon?

No question
But later David
Quint

Puts failure
Inside success

Can't tell
Whether we're inside
Or outside the horse

Capital's innards' movements
Its perpendicular powers
The restless augury
Wanting the rest of the arrow
Its Zeno sum
Back there feathered-ness.

⁚⁚

Spring means
Many things
And thongs

Spring work
For me
On the land

Gives the illusion
Of permanence
All around change

Therefore another big dog
Tail flagging and unflagging
By the window

Arm of a girl
Goes out
Into obvious
Leash

Therefore the seed
Unburies itself

Looks both ways
At the two absent seeds
Saint Augustine stretched thin
Forever

Which means purely
The means of production

Me and my implied
Implement hat

Crows caw
I mean putt putt
Along side their sheens.

::

He bends down
In a kind of prayer
Before the slip of the letter
Publick toilet

Licks the rim
Of the bowl

Therefore he accepts
The way the cops
Spill out of their uniforms

The gate coming down
Like theatre curtains
On the lions

Their bad breath
No movie just now.

∷

I forget to control
The hockey game
By watching

They're so nice
The way they fight
The old way
My way
With bones
And hammers

Ice shavings
Melting
On the glass

I've come
To feed the underdog
But he likes vicious double axels
Therefore dog.

::

Why would you
Wear a tie

That embodies
Looseness
Tethered just enough
To make
Looseness?

Therefore at sixty-four
I find it hard
To get down
To what I weighed
In grade eight

I liked my grade six
Teacher
And way in
Proceeded to weigh in

So she embarrassed me
In front of the class
For being a smart Alec
Which had been surpassing
In grade four

The grade five teacher
Was ready to condemn
The whole class
Because of me
My wintergreen liniment

Just who
Was sucking
Not up?

I got outside the smell to smell
The crime I could save her

And though she herself smoked
Her mother was
The district health nurse.

::

Another limper
Limps by
In this ski town
Not that I think
They shouldn't fall
For it

Just as the mountain
Has freed up its expression

Gives clouds
The mouse
That frightens them back

A ten-foot femur
Skids back
To the drawing board

The wind whips off
The molecules
Therefore the mysterious chill

The cast off elephants
Make all the more room.

::

Today of all
Diminishing days
Or cumulous clouds

It's any
The girls running the hills
Or the hurls
Running the gills

Are more
Than I can
Shake a stick at

Are girls evolved
For hills?

Ezra Pound
Up to no good
Up to his mistress
On the hill
Behind the house
And wife

Noticed the working women
Loads on the their heads
Climbing and so
Callipygian

All he wanted
Was a seat in the *periplum*
"A room of one's own"
And some young
Admiring American poets
To talk to.

::

*Language as the product of an individual is
an impossibility. But the same holds true for
property.*

KARL MARX, *Grundrisse*
(Penguin Classics edition, p. 490)

Now you're back
From where the media
Don't shine

The good news is
You can have
Your old doom back

Therefore
Your money is
On us.

::

Is it him
Or me?
Well

I didn't mean
To start off
So radical alter

I want to be
More popular

Which could be
Taken likewise
Revealing

Naturally I think
It's him

Not so much
He psychologizes per se
But so soon
Off the mark

I mean
Well
Maybe I mean
To mean
Well
And that's all
There is to it

But really
I like to figure out
What's going on
Right down
To the last detail

Well
Not exactly
A last detail

Unless you raise it
To the military sense
The movie made
So much of

Anyway the better
To eat you
Well
No

The better to be
The ego
He would fault me for

The more that ego
Cracks
And the stars
Are real stars

Imaginarily
Dropped out
Of their fixity
And dancing as if
I were thinking them so
And thus

Will-lessness, willfulness
Or Chinese ancient
Willingness
Who knows

The ego
Not in a neuro-
Structural sense

But in a boring
Ordinary little
Hollywood sense
Is nevertheless
Shifty
And happily unpopular

Letting the real stars
Shine
As long as
They don't get
Too uppity

Well again
(As Peter Ustinov
The embezzler
In *Hot Millions*
At the end
Refused
Then accepted
"Weeeell, treasurer")
Uppity
Okay

As long as we all
Get melted
And therefore get
To boot up again
Rich
In a twinkle
Of the eye
Of the needy
Come all
Little Hollywood
A part.

::

Walking down Bear
Street
Animal
Dislocated
With the little big
Buildings
Footing the mountains
And creating
The fall of grace
Up to the structure of
Space
As it allows it to be

I am the devastated
Taxpayer

The local development
Has cost me
Everything

Therefore this is
Absurd

Somebody's nobody
Plans

Have become
Unintentional
Piecemeal

I couldn't have planned
It better
Now that I mansion it

Put the hill
On the pile.

::

I might say
I've had one too
Many Oh Henry! bars

Ones gone bad
Just because they were good

But that is not
What I meant at all

Rolled up
In my trouser leg
Are the rice grains
Of the Chinese food
I said I was
Going to cut out
After a night of drinking

Therefore I must have
Been drinking

But I don't think
Oh Henry! bars
Are the problem

Problems are
The problems

Not that I expect
A life without them

I *want*
Them!

It's just
That problems
Are two-faced

Behind your back
One thing

In front
Another:
Delicious

Only because
You know them
As what
Can turn around
And bite you

You want me
To say
"In the ass"
But here
This would be
Exactly
Up front
And tasteless

Think of something
Else then
Because it
Oh Henry!
Is

Which is
The problem
Unreconstructed

The it
Girl
If ever
There was one.

::

Take
My wife

You can't
Ha ha

She's already
Taken

The kicker
Being
By definition
Not by me

Or anyone

Therefore she is
Death by wife.

⁘

There's Cascade Mountain
On which Dennis Burton
Saw a face

Well I wipe that off
But it's so long since
The mountain talked up
Its birth
Which of course
Is only yesterday
Or mid nineteenth century
Say James Hutton
Who expressed these things
Raw there accurately

A kind of murder
Of its birth well after the fact

So now all these faces
All pretty wrong
Although right in their reflections
Of those wrong reactions
And I can't wipe them down
To the birth
Under the murder

Walter jet-booted
Down the scree
Over a cliff
He foresaw
Especially looking up at the sky
Out of breath

He body-surfed down the rest
Of the way and then crawled
And hobbled to the highway
Lay on the shoulder
With a pen light
Till a cab stopped
And gave him a pillow

He's still out there
After some five or six years

Somebody feeds him
I go out, chat away in the roar
Maybe bend down and lift a sandwich

Of course he takes time off
With his new pelvic plate
Lies there as a rule
For only four or five hours a day.

::

The sun shines
Over the top
Of the establishment
I'm in

Hits the mirror windows
Across the street
Then abandons back
Into the bar

When I pour
My own coffee
In the intense light

The splashes
Are the madness
Of landing on the sun
Rime of the rim

A curator's soup dripped
Down into the soup
Then bounced back up
To her angular nose

We'd been planning
A reading series
Not this mushroom drop
Blown up to what's not
A regular realism
Not always that able

Full of hidden holes
Notably Sterne's big bang
And yawning regression
So beloved by Karl Marx

But there having lunch
I howled at the moon
Deflowered but fresh
With analeptic pock marks.

::

What's so wrong
About backassward

Nothing
I guess

Of course
(the pun)

You can
Choose your past

And you can
Be ready
For anything

But then
Again

When she said
She was trying
To be passionate
About

The gods
Of the culture
Ice climbing
Jazz piano, etc.

I knew
This was not
Religion talking

By which I mean
Religion
In its true
Fundamental
Backasswardness
Talking

But a sure sign
Of the death
Of a sign

Look for a sign
But know instead

Therefore better you
Hide

In the action
Between the keys
And your ear drums

Between your ears
Is between you and you
Until your *I* pokes out
Conducting the music
Back to us bums
Holed up in our seats.

⁚⁚

He's got things to do
I've got things
In a limited period

Yet we would
Enjoy a glass
A meal
And a chat

It's foreordained
And circling
The control tower

And funny how
It is landing
Without us
Like the joke
About fighting
And starting
Without me
Us in this
Case closed

Therefore in time
We will have to
crash the party.

::

Group of couples
Walking on the paved path
Following the river
Unjumped into

They look like tourists
And are

Not conducting
Socratic dialogues

But seem to have
Superseded
Their genitals

Judging by
The smirks
Definitely not there

Not even the one
They hoped otiosely
From me

Hanging by
Reciprocal arms
They weigh in
Less than two

Therefore there are
Two river beds
In the wilderness
Just waiting
To fulfill them

Rivers of course
Condense the sky

Then the big picture
Comes out the taps and toilets

Into curve
The beatitude steps
Once twice thrice

So steeps
So smirks
The straight-faced river.

::

I draw a circle
Around you

And you me
And not long
Before we become
Heavenly bodies
In the worst way

I listen to you talk
And what you say
Hasn't enough escape velocity
So it's Pluto
For you
Like Plato
With egg on his face
The omelette your revolution
Can never make

Now take Marx
Not a Danish cartoon
You would agree

And not an asteroid
That luckily missed us
Or now seems to have
Or so it seems to some
In sum

What's to be done
Is crack this sky rock
Like the heart
Of nineteenth-century Europe

Put your incisors
Into the incisive
Goal-grounded sarcastic
Writing at the centre
Of his own progress

In the grind
Of the argle-bargle
Yes there is
A spectre

Capitalism's adaptive critique
Open heir shadow

Take the earth
From the moon's camera
And of course
It becomes the congealed
Anti-blue cheese

Therefore what we've got
Is Don Quixote
Falling on his lance
If you can get the hang of that
Like a timeless butterfly
But flapping a wing
In the post-contemporary

Undoing the progress
Expanding or slowly exploding
The asteroid right back
To Tristram funny Shandy
Out of joint
With his deeply Danish
"Now cracks . . .
Angels sing."

::

Okay perhaps five minutes ago
Or a day and a half
I divined the action
Of the particle
If you can call it that
That grounds
(Its self-grounding notwithstanding)
The nature of mass

But
As luck would have it
It's slipped my mind
Since I didn't
Oh-so nineteenth-century
Write it down

More importantly
I probably looked down upon
The service truck
Dressed like a wound
With snow

With snow
For the reason
The cunning of reason
To truck its own earlier
Into a later proof

Proof of the earlier
Fir trees
The truck squeezed under
Writing the snow straight
On its back
But carrying like a Labrador
Burrs from the pasture
On its tail
Little boughs
Little green bough wows
Laurels
And hardy har

Through the window
A window of time as we say
To the intentionality of trees
And Ernie Kroeger lifting
The wild writing of pine beetles

The lasting confessions
The distended record
Broken

Pro and contra
The cliché.

::

He knows he should ask
In respect to basic civil society
About what preoccupies him
And not, don't say it, formally
The coordinates of civil society itself

Wonders not whether a woman would
But if her necessarily self-consciousness
Differs from his own

Therefore his calculation
Reflected into and out
Of a her and now

Jacks him out of
Nothing in particular

Into a heady feeling

Don't say
It's all good

When the famous climber
Drinker-in of the upward downward
Asked her
Volunteered as a shuttle bus
Driver
If she were a climber

I told her to have said
"Just a social climber."

::

A hockey player
Without a stick

A TV
That drops the gloves

My nephew
In another town
Puts on that cyber glove
That hands him
The stick

Shakespeare spears
The Globe
That rinky dink
One step ahead of the default map
Itself one step if a million

You are infighted
To the theatre of war

Therefore by any other name
The two globes
Both imaginary but different
And problematically related
Are fighting it out

Kabob's your uncle
A pun that falls apart
For the play without the play.

::

The relation of simple
To complex
Is not simple

Which does not mean
Complex wins

Simple has important moments
For survival
And not going mad

He said re the poetry
Of this world
He wasn't into complexity

Therefore I know
Why he left
A coconut on my desk

I looked at it
Gave it a shave
The phrenology
Proceeded on its own
And so did the real
Science

As punishment
The conditions for coconut
Are made to kiss unto eternity
Just as Wyndham Lewis

Would have the lovers
In *The Human Age* stuck
To their guns
Pickled tink in their gums.

::

D'ya ever imagine
The insight that got away
And that left the bartender
With his back to you
Talking to a pretty girl
Could be more important

Than the insight
That didn't give up the ghost

You could say
The insight that got away
Is not the elephant in the room
Or as a wit a whit above
The cliché incidence
Would say
"The gorilla in the room"

Therefore it is
An *ele-illa*

Rogue letters
Proved up
To gone spirits.

::

I crossed the road
On the bridge over the Bow River
In Banff
Where especially there are
No parked cars
Which tend to compromise
A sidewalk's inner face

Therefore in the middle
On the asphalt
Ranging down
On the approaching commercial van
I couldn't shake the sacred
From my broken-in running shoes
Cross trainers
Interpellated by the catalogue
Heard round the world

At any rate
Hesitating for a moment
The shoes were not good enough
For the asphalt

That kept emerging
From the tar and crushed rock

Quite an empirical miracle
Undermined and underpinned
By that van

Or a fifty-pound kid
On a twenty-pound bike
Going twenty-five kilometres an hour
In a three-second zone
Even if crowded out
To the spirit sidewalk

I walk on air
Like the out-sorcerers claim
The tar and the crushed rock
Import themselves
Dignity therefore driven up
Without a shovel
Or even the rest of the Cheshire cat.

::

Here I am
With a little steno pad
Floating I can't figure out
Whether on a chunk of ice berg
Or on a bit of Titanic debris

Right over
To a guy who just sat down
At the bar

Not a drunk waiting to happen
Has a mole on the side of his head
Serenely comfortable
In his boney body
Not Scottish
Perhaps kilt a bear
When he was three

You understand we don't
Know this man

Therefore again
The tidal wave
Après ski
Is not so plangent
For this planted gent

A plain gent
I mean without the bells
And Whistler mountain

Because of consumer power
And leaving early
This marginally needy guy

Left with a sizeable chunk
Of the horseshoe bar

A few chairs
Five or sixty bottles of liquor

And after that
A few servers

Tipped themselves off
To the phantom limbs
Of the future.

::

She said to the nasty critics
The poems were
But poor flowers

And I said
His boat with poem
Its cargo

Would not quite work
On the boulevarde

Notwithstanding the aura
The flower on flower

Insect feelers
Crickets say
Two sticks rubbing
It in the bush
Boulevarde

He embraced
The boy scout fire
I couldn't hazard
To argue

But I did point out
With a stick of my own

It was their sticks
He was rubbing
The wrong way

Even lightning
In the remote forest
Its invading smoke

Though spectacular
Is not good enough

He replied
And what he said
Was what they said

So I was in
Deep shit
Or manure
The gardening mothers
Of the fifties used to say
With relish

Therefore
Roses are red.

⁑

I have an ache
For chocolate gan*ache*
Nash my Ogden

I have an ache
For the perfume
In the elevator
Because I know
Whose it is

Twice removed
I have neither the cake
Nor have I eaten it

I like the corner
Rather than
What's around it
Therefore my mistake
Is absolute.

::

I could say
Something's not here

But then if here
Is anything
It's all here

I mean it though
Something's not here
By which I mean
Not these words
Wherever you are
But a "physical place"
To be gone
I won't mention
Will I Mr. Noah the funnel
Run aground?

Course already it
The unnameable
As in heavy duty allusion
But also as in
The afore-unmentioned
Is here

Therefore
The tabletop
Certainly not arborite
I suppose I have
Nothing against
Especially since my old landlady
Gave me that such topped table
Plus bed and dresser
When I had to get out
Before shall we say the bulldozer

Is not all
But suggests
But what?

Do you mind?
But long ago
I went hunting
For the perfect slingshot
Damned every tree in the yard
With a gaze
That loved them
More than they would care to think
Though not more loved
Than a bird out of the derived ground
Expressed as a dead duck

The slingshot was there
Just not in the actual branches

Therefore Goliath
Becomes David
Only smaller

Sommelier
Becomes
The nose
Just a name away

Like Transylvania
If you take the cobwebs
As stringed instruments
Making quiet
A bracket.

::

Because he irritated me
Purely relative to me
Being open to it
I deemed him an asshole
Or worse wherever you might find
That particular figure

It is crude
Especially since he was more
Nerd or in a local way, star
Quite popular for reasons
I won't go into
And that will pass
Into other reasons
For other outcomes

An irritation rises
To murderousness easily
And it did

So the next time
He landed I contracted
A hired "gun"
As I was
Too lazy to bother myself

Therefore just as the weapon
Was about to engage
I looked at his thoughtful face
Listening to a young
Enthralled woman
Or one with some sympathy left over
For the wit he enjoyed in himself

And I pulled the plug
Not on the hired killer
They probably got on
The guy was charming
If you live on that planet
And you do
If you have to get close enough
For a shot

But on myself
Therefore down the drain
I am
On myself

It doesn't mean
That I'm full of love
For the people
That cloud over our hamlet
Really a village
Changing into hens and hacksaws
And camels

It means I'm there for them
In the sense condensed
From the figures above

My door is not open
Which is surprising.

::

Right off
No *point d'appui*

For what?
It remains

Whatever the position
The form, content
The thing methinks
It doesn't just float

Mechanisms assault
Chemism's bases
And acids, salts
Are uploaded in order
To undermine

Methinks the cushions
Deal with the crashes
And the chemism
Can't put its finger on
What it can't put its finger on
Conversations enter
My head
Circle around like crows
A carcass

Therefore I'm dead
Serious
And inhuman to boot

If I arise
But not but
Or if

I arise and go now
Not only not to the tobacconist

I don't sloppeth around
Or damn God

I walk down along the river
And the dog barks at me
More to see if I react
Recognize him chained up

I tell him
And his ceilinged barks
I've heard it all before

But on the way back
He barks on barks
Turning his head from the TV
Where he'd been watching Sartre
In his living room going on about
A dog's recognition of his lack
Of speech
Therefore in the living room there
The epitome of boredom

On the river bank
The barking
Not a bad idea

Backing out of the human
Taut chain or loosed learning

Speech's lack
Back.

::

Twenty years ago
From the sky hook

The local CBC radio call-in show
In my tractor
Put me off
Till music damned me
That Shavian booze
A walking snooze

So the talk show
Till we drown

Therefore God loves them
And after hours and days
Round and round
The field

I listen to the symptoms
And know I'm sicker
Than these ghost callers

So I guess in this significance
Of sins
I take God's points
As they diffidently
And worldly other become me.

::

Running around like a naked ape
Blinds closed
A closed affair
Nevertheless
A full-fledged pervert
Jiggling around
No clothes
All in half light

Pitter-pater of big feet
A light slap on the thigh
With the penis
Not sure what to do with itself

Ostensibly caught between
States, i.e., the body owner-operator
And so authorized

Therefore the slide to perversion
Changed the room
Into a change room
Sliding off into the California Pacific

Well I'm wearing the ocean
The fur-covered piano wavering
In the depths.

::

He lives in the itch
In the cells of his muscles
Encouraged as they are

His uniform is in his skin
Cut up by football equipment
Under it

He wants to talk
All talk needs a bias

Or like the perfectly ambidextrous
Has to jump into the street
With both feet together
When the walk sign alights

Therefore Mr. McLuhan
Everything is eaten
Drawn down to the menu
By the low hanging
Blue-veined bicep
Beautiful as a startling breast.

∷

Cracking the raw eggs into the bowl
Saving the yokes for disposal

Abortion rears itself
On the radio
It's loaded phonemes

Therefore we gather secondary
The gardener
His/her chosen people.

::

Fertilizer truck driver
Taps his calculator
Introjects his GPS

Drags me
A vampire anyway
Into the internet

Anhydrous ammonia
Hisses, escapes a bit
So our eyes water
Against an ultimate
Water shortage

Therefore 9/11
Can't be repeated enough

After all
It pales in comparison
To itself

Therefore Peter Dale Scott's trail
Is to porridge liable
Not too hot
Not too cold.

::

A family displaced anyway
I guess eh
In a tourist town

Camping as slumming
As parody
But here the parody
Sinks into a cutting edge arising
Through a plate tectonic shift
In the unconscious

The prominent father leading
The entourage
Looking over the patio
Through the open doors
Into the sexy lounge
Coloured lights and qualified music
As opposed to quality music
Not that it necessarily isn't

The father of course
On the edge
Embedded in the family
Perhaps even the in-itself glue

But then of course
On the boundary
And a little extra
On the side

The father
Taking in
Through the doors
The scene

Therefore
I meet his eyes
Don't flinch
Become the father
Of the father
Who needs me now
More than ever.

::

If you'll let me detach
The politically incorrect term "cripple"
From the misheard creek
Or babbling song

I ask therefore
Why do these cripples
Come to this
Famous ski town?

Why does this
Beautiful "hole"
Quoted most especially
In the orgasm
That stays on the chair lift
When you get off

Why between the up and down
Backward gravity
Is the jury — out?

::

The mountains are not sick
Or Thomas Mann manned

But they micro climate are
And tease

Down south and east
If you get my drift
The snow drifts abound

Therefore I tarry
In the sun
Some put on shorts
And the tank tops
Go nicely with Robert Frost's
Fire and ice
Hot house suspension
Bridge

And yet yeti
Saskatchewan nudge nudges
Alberta
Which springs forward
Into super province

Hockey over time
Chases the educated dog
As his heart gears down
To the useless glue
Of his blood
Out there
Beyond the fringe
As my mother and aunt
Used to laugh with
Not having read brave Hegel
Who told the trans-parent sun
To go away
Come here.

::

Two elderly women
At the bar celebrating
I overhear

Therefore I let them speak
To and for themselves

Lie on the couch
Forty-six years ago
Sick with the flu
See the ceiling as floor
The stippling as cracks
In the parched earth

But what fun
Climbing over the lintels

Running the quarter mile
Faster than ever
The next day at the meet

Not knowing the secret
This lucky late break
In the training
Released
Me from trying

Turning things over
To getting behind them
Seconds to none

No gravity
On the now timely
Sistine Chapel
Going nowhere
Fast.

::

Wine right into the marrow
Of your bones what else
Is too much wine
And the brain has to run
With it

The bartender and servers
Respond as you mention
The penumbra the way drunks
Get themselves classified with token
Differences proving the rule
But not making the servers testy
Just more efficient negotiators
Though they do appreciate
With the tips the tipsy margins

As long as the curve ball
Swerves back to the mixed-up box
On the money so to speak
You can speak your mind
That bottled enterprised genius

Around the rocket
Out to smash the mirror
Already there
Ahead of the light.

::

You walk a mile in your own shoes
And can't get used to it

The strange thing is
You skate over this secondary fact

Same as where you are walking to
Doubled up on your focus
The goal is not so much weak
But neither is it a shoe-in
In terms of a saturated motive

Not looking good
So lucky the sky arching over
In dutiful happiness
You can't touch
Deep into you

Can always turn your back
Especially as you hover over
The words skating over one another
And that you can stop and ask
Word of mouth directions
Still as from afar

On a long weekend beginning
Go east out of Banff
Watch the cars
On the other side of the median
Driving backwards

On Monday watch them driving east
Right way around
As you route the kernel back
Into peak-unpeak time
All talk and geophysics
Flying off the deep sea shelves.

::

They think well of him
Based on what
They bring to the table
And on what he holds back
Yet perhaps doesn't have anymore
Or in a way never did
Coming to this

He of course runs with it
Runs by this window
As a work

This other guy thinks ill of him
Based on what else
But envy
Crazy as that is
Saddled with geometry

A deduction
That holds up it seems

So much seems
That on his back
He feels the heat of hate
Bore in
Such is the training

Between ill and well
He somewhere lies
But he doesn't lie
Not when he's sleeping

But when he awakes
Leaves the bed
For the cloud computer.

::

Take her
Walking by every day
Doing her job

Pretty lit up
And foxy
I took a shine

At my age oh yeah
"Just watch me"
As we go far and war
If we can take the trouble

Then she's downgraded
To a pleasant planet
Seasoned sensation

Then she's gone
Just like the little newspaper shop
Just like the forty-year-old bookstore

Sheila Watson was right after all
Off a duck's back
For an old hat on the new
I.e., freshman saying
"So what's new?" to her
Without the question mark
Big deal *transience*
John Donne done

Takes a while to pick out
The stays back the figure of time

Therefore
The walk across a field
The walk through the mall
With its sea weed hands
Out of the fire into the wok

Or the silk worm
Or the spider building out
Into a nothing
Atop the tent

So again I'm weathered
Wiped clean
Just in time producer
At home on the genome.

::

Each night up to bed
Is the big bad night
For the kid you try to kid
Then flat as a cat on the mat
For many a year
Except for the booze
And some succubi

Finally it's like nothing's settled
Therefore you settle down
While everyone else
Wants to settle up
Even though you know
They're dead to the world

You go on killing them
Over and over anyway

In the morning
You're so bloody tired
And there's just one tree
In the yard
Silhouette or an hour of hoar frost
Or leaves that turn over
To that two-tone green

The rhizomes are gone
With the saint's underground snakes
The spayed academy's scented book
Treats you the customer you are
Always right

Just as sowed
Are all the wrongs right

The negative's open
Reserved delight.

::

You go here
You go there
You walk into a place
Square peg in a round hole
And so you proverbially
Grind off the edges

Set your reader
On the counter
Like hanging guns up
In those westerns

The reader reads
On its own

So you're fine
Till the guy comes up
Relates you to some of his
Quite hifalutin connections
You must meet

Therefore the guns and reader
You would have to take off
Would be like garbage
During a garbage strike
On the street

The real problem
Is those edges
And what kind of world anyway

She comes over drawn
By your edginess
Which in actuality
Sticks out like a broken femur
Through your jeans
Not like a nice hard on
Makes her edgy

She's so tired after a long night
Serving the public
Which feeds her her lines
She longs to lie down
On the piled garbage

In fact checks out each bag
On the sidewalk
Is nothing but defense mechanisms
As she crosses them off
One by one

She walks down the sidewalk
And vanishes
Well is swept off her feet
By a headless horseman
Who exchanges her for
Not a body without organs
But a body without bills.

::

I wake up from a nap
Hadn't realized how long I was
Feet well into the rest of the room

The atmosphere's still
One atmosphere psi wise

Those correlatives Eliot was
Going on about
Are all part of it

Makes us into helpless idiots
Apparently the word "idiot"
Quite once a social classist term

Going down to get the paper
I heave the airplane wing
From the driveway onto the marigolds

Sarkozy's dad quite a sensation
In the art world
Looking awry

The best novelist ever
On the CBC talks like an idiot
As you might expect
Despite correcting the clichés
As you might expect

The new clichés reaching out a hand
Like that to Johnson
His whetted dictionary
The Scottish eat

I kick the tires of the police car
Cop a feel
Frisky I'm frisked

Therefore you can joke about anything
Depending on the institution
Or the media
Spiralling through the melted widgets
I mean idgets.

::

Of course not a lot of us
Have valets anymore
I let mine go last week
Sorry two weeks ago

As if numbers
Could make a joke
They can with a voltage drop
In the abided by axioms
Or rather within the open pen
They underwrite

Therefore a party politician
Is not dropped but draped
From the high-rise
x floors up

A couple of hackers hack in
To the back of him

They dine out on their find
Hardly headlines

Way too sophisticated and seminal
And incongruous for the first page
Or editorial or witty grammar letters

Basically they have a new computer
That hacks back
Telling them more than they want

They love him
Like a lame duck author
Who doesn't give a shit
Has calibrated his fine self
Out of a twelve gauge job
That has no description.

::

The Christian religion was able to be of assistance in reaching an objective understanding of earlier mythologies only when its own self-criticism had been accomplished to a certain degree, so to speak, potentially. Likewise, bourgeois economics arrived at an understanding of feudal, ancient, oriental economics only after the self-criticism of bourgeois society had begun.

KARL MARX, *Grundrisse*
(Penguin Classics edition, p. 106)

A bird blew by
Outside the patio doors
Was the scene to be seen

It had an arrow
In its beak
Which made for the apperception
In the first place

Arrow and bird
In mutual interception
Although I'm sure
There was a bias

All this as I put my vodka
Down on the piano
When the sonata picked up
In a most syncopated way
The swan's swan song
Scholars come down

The pianist quite high strung
No more prima donna
Than usual
Ignored my outré act
Since the scholars agreed
I was a documented drunk

Confined to this niche approval
I birthed out
With some Chinese gibberish

Doctors said it was a function
Of an earlier migraine
Worse than the migraine
Regarding immediate commerce

I re-entered from the other wing
On the note of an inexpertly
High-pitched fart
A Delmore's delight
Which could be a hidden reference
To a Montreal place of smoked meat

Or simply to a kid looking
At the obscure rain
Superimposed on the grade one reader
Depicting a school girl
In her yellow rain gear

Through the translucent glass
In the doctor's office
Like a basement
Half sunk in the sloping earth

The page turner asked if
I had a reed in that thing

I said I sure did have
A dark red hemorrhoid
Like a tonsil or a tooth
Was the therefore Nixon.

::

Now that I live in Stockholm
Where the houses all around
Have functioning eave troughs
That convert to pop guns
And other transformer princes

I'm not at all surprised
At the big "semi" gas truck
Not jake-braking
But gunning around the corner
Where saplings become trees are

Therefore the village is octopied
Slapped on the bum old-handedly

Put on by the centre
That can't but be put
On hold
Sent screaming
Through formula one
Motions
Where the tumble weeds
Without architraves
Never came
Before us.

::

The shoe's on the other shoe
My feet have bunions
In themselves are onions

Shoe on shoe is two skin beginning
You get my point however
My nineteenth-century English
Trying to disarm the twenty-first
With cracker barrel cracks

Was chatting with an Italian
In a first degree (or perhaps second)
Remediation

I had no idea those guys
Were so smart
Despite the Renaissance
And the piggy-backed Christians
Where it wouldn't make any difference
To say "piggy-backing Christians"

With one shoe per foot
I meant to plod along
With expressions of irony
That everyone could relate to

I'm talking to you claquers
Applauding with your eyebrows
Before I get it all out

Therefore the kids with their stand
On the sidewalk eschew
Cheap lemonade
Offer cut-rate condoms
That could have precluded them
They proclaim
Therefore I stop for Alices and Emilys
Which they don't have

You're impossible I say
Out of my depth
But looking down

They pull out all the stops
Can't help they got fucked up.

‡

It is my theory
That this house is cooler
When the wind is blowing
When below a certain temperature
The outside temperature
Is nevertheless quite a bit warmer
Than often is the case
In winter

Because rushing around the house
The air becomes a low pressure system
And sucks outside the warm air

Therefore I shall be looking
For the leakages
Properly sealing them

This is a lovely old house
With a dear old den

The agriculture we do
Is outside the moat

I go to the first seed
In the first row
Ignoring the seeds spilled
Around the front of the shop
Where we adjust the seeder

They are scattered on the gravel
And dry dirt
Will sprout if you look at them

But I tell you telluric
They're just interstellar gas
Either planted point of origin
Or beyond my grasp
I shell my Shelley thoughts
Take the ions aplenty by the horns.

::

Right after a haircut I find
You look so secondary
Even tertiary
Not hard done by
Just done by

Like a lapped Mennonite
In running shoes

Even though you're coiffed
And taken care of
Whether or not you induced it
You're still living by your wits

The link at the liquor store
Requires a surplus stumble and recovery
Working the tip of your tongue

When you finally get away
From these menial links
To where it's happening
The temptation is there
To grab the inspissator
For the unitary bottle
You put yourself in
On the model ship
But the murky bottle that inverts
You and your priorities
Is only a taste to die for
Later in the night life
Just before the night

The links as new techno peasant work
Give way to broken strata
Heaved up into virtual mountains
Complications you can take or take to
The anthropogenic sublime

As we sidle almost but not quite
Up to the machines as Karl would have it
I saddle up with the salmon
Swim and fly the river ladder

Leaving the cities far enough behind
Or ahead to be contained
And slid out to sea
The predominant orange
Sodium vapour lights
Lowered by the great curvature
The widened louche eye picks up

Over the learning curve
But harder
In usually dry northern Texas
Mary Ann attends in a stall
Curly's laminitus

The trial-running war planes
For prospective buyers
With their cannon and missile cases
Ear split the sky and the barn
Turning on a bank computer dime
Back to Carswell
On the northern edge of Fort Worth
To the air base abandoned up
To a manufacturer

"I could see the rivets, smell the space age alloys
and the hyped up Avgas. I could feel
my molecules dissociate"

Therefore the Gadsden Purchase
Down and to the right
New Orleans honking
Acadia going down too
The counterfactual French
On another plane

The wet winter
The too sweet grass
(Not the source after all
Of Curly's fatal infection).

::

When I use old expressions
Like "everything's up to date in Kansas City"
For Canadian content
Minus the Canadian

Do you think it's like
Home cooking
If that's indeed any kind of desideratum
You say hegemony or bio-politics
Too many times
And they reach for their *tertium quid*

You know those farmers
Aren't stuck in their gum boots
Otherwise on to which crested wheat heads
Are dried in turn

They're crunching out
The difference between
The general relativity effect
And the special relativity effect
Folded into the satellite GPS information
As they go around the irrigation pivot
Dodging bombs
Before the pivot's up
The païntbrush
As if out their ass
Swathing colour field the screen

Time speeding up so far
From the earth
Slows down with the orbit speed
But they don't cancel
They love this stuff
Like they love their secret tool drawers
As can they figger a double entendre

They'd light their cigarettes
With a powerful magnifying glass
Just to be corny hybrid
And self-embedded
If they still smoked that is

Gadgets flock to the fields
Like geese

I ride the elephants
While the tigers leap
At my dangling feet

When I get off the satellite
My legs are longer
But still don't reach
The barycentre by a lot of whiskers
And I don't jump
Since my joints are out of joint
Where I hide drugs
And near perfect ball bearings
Relatively speaking

Behind the old cinder brick shop
We pile up machines one
On top of the other

Therefore I hunker down with match
And do the dog-whistle

Of course they won't burn
All that steel shined up
By the abrasive dirt

Though the rust is slow fire
And the fire "rapid rust"
As John over there in England wrote

The ants say
And I've said this before
The littlest fire is always too big

Yet people
Fools for imperative ends
Their Hobbesian habits not Hobbits

Are always trying
To start something
Or spit into a beer can
Through the eye
Of the baffled air.

::

My nephew said
My brother's wife said
Asparagus grows good
In a dead horse patch

The *Globe* said
If you're gonna drink wine
Eat lots of asparagus

Therefore give me the nice cab
Of yore
Hold the horses.

⁘

I'm leaning way over the fence
With all the other physicists
At the horse track
Looking for the accelerated particles
To come smashing down
The home stretch

No. 5's jockey has his knees
Especially high up around his ears
Riding as he is on an alligator
Strickly a mudder
Joke I read in an old *Playboy*
I bought strictly for the swell beavers
I thought I saw
We call *Canada's History* now

James Michener turned to James Jones
From Here to Eternity, Some Came Running
On a talk show
Said they'd both be forgotten
Jones a big fellow slouched down
And harumphed

Most workshops have got rid
Of their lathes
Are busy writing now
And I've found first hand
They're doing more than all right
Setting out the purloined culture
In excess of the adjustable jig table

Therefore I jump on my bed
Poor man's trampoline
The people downstairs
Think it's Baroque sexual prowess.

::

Walking down the street under the maples
His gait goes giddyup whoa
To a cadenced thought thought through
Retracing its immanence
Arcing over the stutter of trees

He shuns the precipitous horizon
Which when you think of it
Is right
Even and especially were it a bomb
Come ironically home to roost
In someone's garage which happens
At least on the radio relays

The question is
When should you listen to the radio
The one with the gravamen hits?

Certainly not in the kitchen which is a where
Sorry, yes in the kitchen
When you're having breakfast
But not after when you've moved
To a room of one's own

Radio and what gets beyond the phatic
Though not the voice of war we huddle around
The phatic always takes its sweet revenge

At least where I'm about to pose
I mean propose
As the best splash down
Or give of the glove
From a hard throw
From the voice of an authority
The counter authority
Cominatchya as if it were
AM radio and phatic revenge
It may as well be

Seeding wheat and performing the working
No plugged hoses no weeds on the shanks
Tank good for fifty acres
Or a couple of hours

The predictable
Though at a high level
Commentary
Filling your ears
Is a pollination
Devoutly to be wished

Therefore I turn off the radio
See the tide go out with the gulls

Events scratched into earth
Retarded
Put in the germinating way
A production going beyond me
Into the season's end

The radio is hard work
And a long day
Somebody's got to do it

Keep giving
Undecisionistic ground

Then on the air wave
Pirate the ballerina

Peel off
The pirouette

Whirl and fix
Whirl and fix

Round after dusty round
Exorcize
The wound-up owl.

::

Going back in the mists of time
Back in the most of time
Back not in the mast
But the tall ship of time
The tall ship that sinks
In the must-hear aesthetic tones
In thus this widening pool

That little pinch
A couple of millennia ago
After the best biologist
For the most of the next millennia
After Confucius who set down some rules
Of thumb for the opposable set
After perhaps the asteroid
What, a billion or three years ago
Delivered the organic goods

That that little pinch Jesus Christ
Has sunk in
Is very odd

Therefore I unbutton
Not all the good
Just unbutton
Slide and slide
The sipperyest slope
A free fall
"Beyond good and evil"

I'm not talking fancy
Existential structures
Or a worlding process
Or different species of time
You know how our before and after
Is supposedly after
Tellingly again
A superior before and after
That's all at a distended once upon

I'm just lazing
Into a dumb scientist's lit up lids-up eyes
Gawking down the bowling alley
Where all the pins are mist

Explained away in the guttering mind
As true as straight
As the stacked decades in the warehouse
As the crunched bums in the whorehouse.

::

Here's this eunuch
Eating his donair with either sauce
Once so lonely he came out
The other side and turned it into
Not the oldest profession
But a regular going concern
Congruent with what the *The G & M*
Social Studies stats said about
Happiness rearing its fixed-income face
For singles just about the time they retire

And now with his surplus concern
In a power wrap of social awareness
His heart breaks for the young couple
About to try breaking up their marriage

It seems the needle in their haystack
Flicks to stable then wildly to unstable
On the rim of a latest topology

Does the eunuch really care
In any substantial way
That would compute
For a possible not just utopian society
That would fold in some other
Bells and whistles
Some really necessary
Like machinic governors
Some for a new kind of enjoyment
That vexes some of the old ironies
Or fly a little easier
The mediation moments?

Or has he just colonized the couple
A comic transference
To dollhouse parents
Both neutered and nice
Like canned laughter obliging

Health food's smarter pre-health food
Therefore just gathered

A steal
Into the soul
The Lady of Mirror's *mir.*

::

My grandfather Smeaton
Labour MLA
Wouldn't cross the floor
To accept Aberhart's offer in 1935

My uncle brilliant with numbers
Eccentric and absent-minded
Foremost tax expert in the West
Wouldn't in the Aberhart government ledger
Write road grader for Cadillac
So quit

He used to drive through an orange light
Almost red
And say, "That cuts off the traffic behind"

But now, say the cars cut off at the intersection
Represent consequent pollution
And climate change

And the grandfathered cars that made it
Are simply a world
Of nostalgia therefore the cupola half
Of Gödel's theorem
That theorem that only humanities types
Entertain and that workin' mathematicians
Pretty well ignore:

Nostalgia, memorabilia, Jubilees, Olympic pins
Hugh Hood inventories
Of small town early last century licorice and candies
Restored automobiles

Put a soft grenade in the cupola
And you've cars all over the place
Immaculate innocuous cars
Cut off tails that drive the economy
Wag wages and put musk in armpits

Put your ear plugs in
And play the air guns
Till your carpal tunnel's
At the end of the light
Make some more robot jokes
About how the robots are getting all
The jokes
A twisted habit you take almost to genre
Whose demands stave off Alzheimer's
And wows the kids coming up
With the heads and shoulders
That are ploughed into feet
Non sequiturs to cars and a step up

Put all the cars
On the head of a pin
Now tell me
These are categorical angels?

The useless ones
That get insinuated into the situation
Itself full of sinful insinuations

There they are oceanic
Committing nothing
Let alone sins

Yet between the hammer
And the loose vibe
They try wing the right thing
Tied and not
Just in time.

::

Take flighty capital
Financial instruments, products
And processes
Parlayed from breathers in and out
Of the so-called base economy
To paper and screens where the eccentric
Shoeless (see Henwood) former physicists
And mathematicians from the academies
Play fascinating games with equations

All fun much poked and pokered at
And dipped into and out of and back into
By the pods hanging on
Yet touching down on soft touch
Superstructural vines of venal vino
Ultra haptic back down
In the base nervous system
Handi-graft slit into the golden throats
Of political apologists and partyers

In Haiti just after the revolution
And before the elites and then aggrieved France
The US marines and IMF

The subsistence farmers grew an array
Of vegetables and fruits
Our new city gardeners
Would kill for

But I quickly add how misplaced
The trope is

We have our ups and downs
In export prairie agriculture here in the north
We retrench and have our periods
Of what the sociologists call self-exploitation

The figure "in our blood"
Does justice to the feeling
Tested but turned
To satisfaction in actual sweat
And grain in the fall in the bins

Is "in your blood" a fair way of talking
About a possible mere addiction?
Back to back to land primitive style
Which at this point in our cities it is
Bought into as

Past the correction of the snorting bulls
And what the adrenaline bears

We therefore have to ask of Hegel and Marx
If they are right that in sum
Mediated place
The immediate earth is not at all backward
For the concrete spirits wanting

The stretch pad or drawing room
Between past and future
The confessions of blood
Troped up and down the distended brain
On the cusp of all time
St. Augustine said no one
Us hicks of haecceity
Makes sense of

While all the while
We think we know.

::

The two of them in the library
Each reading Darwin

They set the books aside
And ask who dares win

Outside they punch the clock
Then clean each other's

So end up in the hospital
Where they sit together over a chess board

They digress into a new labour power
For which they receive no cheque
Or checkmate

Therefore they become doctors
Of Darwinnie the pooh
Evolutionary crapologists

They act as if they're from the future
But are actually patients
In their own GUTS

To put a plug in
For the quantum cosmology theorists.

::

A man kicks back in his recliner
Falls half asleep
Easier done than the half pregnant one
And quite common
These hypnagogic states dating
From the mid nineteenth century
Ballooning out from Oxford

His child self drops out
Down into the spiralling springs
He reaches fecklessly up
To the levers like on home hockey set games
But his manhood deserts him
Even as it requires him

He doesn't even bother to lace his skates
And wonders how he'll ever execute
Among other things, his sexual duties

Therefore notwithstanding he sinks
In his own tank just as much
As the screeching metal tracks run over
And crush him
The tracks themselves celebrating
A split into road
And thing on the road

He is maybe in a better position
Maximally better weakened
To appreciate the cosmetic accoutrements
And fanfare of the womb
Swaying above him

Unless this is a dangerous fetish
That would wake the warrior on ice
Potentially broken water.

::

The kid's voice from 1945
On the radio sixty-five years later

Responding to the interviewer's question
About the end of the war
A sort of overseas with reason
Feeling

The voice high pitched and too movie
For its own good from within
Our theatre

Therefore
Slightly less than a year before
I was born
The kid was hey like next door
A bit of a slouch

The banality
Of Bethlehem
Between
The register.

::

If defamiliarization has to keep
One-upping itself
It's absurd

If it has a limit
Within the historical moment
(Marx's augmented Hegelian usage
Diverted from Newton's mechanics)

Then we realize it's a game
We can learn
Which not so much generates
But betrays
A rightful meta-position

Therefore what we have
Is not a failure to communicate
So much as a dramatic deadlock

The meta-position is unrepresentable
All the better to eat you
Or for to interpret the world
Long way away from changing it

Marx developed an inner logical structure
Long way away from the structure
Of presentation for an audience in mind

The world dynamic with/in history
Can't be presented
Can't be represented

"You read a thousand pages of Hegel's logic
To understand *Capital*'s four thousand pages
And you read eight hundred pages of *Grundrisse*
To understand Hegel"

You kill what you flush/flesh out
Your strategy of subversive syntax
Or non-syntax
The gaps you leave in leaping to more
But only more
Totalled, crashed or summed, totalities
As ideology as "the intersection
Of narrative and cognition"

Or the deft condensed sentences
With the figurative or the abstractions proper
Are all readable and left wanting back-up
Interpretants
Let alone the actants
Devolved to actors

Improv to improve
The social individual

The invisible hand
Reveals a new ethical universal
Pegged in the abyss
Bad i.o.u.

Therefore
No peg
No point at all

No same
No measurable difference.

::

Letter to *Alberta Views:*

I think the reviewer of *Woodstock Rising* (May '10') could be right within "show/don't tell" co-ordinates where her twist of the SDS slogan "more action, less talk" might apply. With McLuhan's often useful "hot/cool" binary she would have *Woodstock* as hot, too detailed. Less detail would draw the reader into a drawing of her own, more action would make it more entertaining. But what if what is of interest here is precisely the hard work of debating issues, measuring events and the looping of macro politics back into micro, in sum the long haul of social action, to untwist "more action"? Wayman's text rimes the minimal modulations of daily "actions," a demanding kind of music whose quantity in time effects a quality beautifully at one with those hard-heady times. Of course the book is not faceless document, but marbled with clashing personalities full of various misgivings but also good humour, where more than one track always plays (love life, grad studies, etc.). The "action parts" work as comedy and suspense, but also, in an imaginary register, as allegory and strange consummation of a hot/cool dialectic that haunted the lived era, one that eventuated in an Eliotic whimper signified in the title of the *Esquire* anthology *Smiling Through the Apocalypse.* The fictional "apocalypse" counter-points as well as raises the pilgrims' progress, as it were, into an uncanny register. The book itself, as Walter Benjamin would have it, blasts an au-thentic and articulated sixties into our time, for which we should be thankful, to have that smile cracked up in this new laughable order.

::

Such a generic night in the spring
Should be seeding wheat
Were it not for the winter-like light
In the light snow, the socked-in clouds

The town lights in the window
Uprooted
A blurred pinpointed night
A contradiction

A flying carpet let's face it
Banking into a turn
Therefore some gravity on the side
The marriage of heaven and hell
Making whoopee a moment of levity

Called up on the carpet
Where the sea figures toss
Crisscross loss of the telos

Now Saturday noon and the clouds
Position overhead like an SF space ship
In this, lowered down to sci-fi
Now no sense of Saturday noon
Collection of arrows
For the primitive quiver.

::

Over there is a shot put
Or simply *shot* we Olympians say

Well now not going too Hamlet
It methinks
Is more like a pumpkin

Is *it methinks* the clue?
Therefore the crime of idealism
Caught ready-handed empty
You have to hand it to it

Okay let's get started
Where is the truth?
In the bush
Or in the hand?

You said it
And then the sentence excuses itself
The ideal mind is a hand
Daniel Dennett puts a dental in it
Then it excuses itself

Okay the truth is up in the air
Empirical enough though the air be
We picture-think here
The air too disappears around the bend
Of the singletree and the risible rhizome

If there's such a thing as truth
And there is I would bet
If you'll excuse the hedge

Then it's not in the pumpkin
Or its seed
Only the truth is real
Said "the mighty thinker"

You think counterintuitive?
You fumble your own fingers
Butter fingers you accuse
And want to recuse

The truth cuts through butter
You butter believe
But wouldn't think
Of denying you your fingers
Nor can it fix the fumbling

The knife is sharp
So is the truth
Only the truth is real
And sharper in reserve
Go figure

The quarks are jammed in the traffic
We deem
In place of the place
Without a helicopter.

∷

You can't state the fact
As if it were in the stating happening
Of a man walking on his patio
Oblivious to the bird overhead
Not a big bird, say owl
But pretty big, say sea gull

You can't state the fact
Well you can
But don't tell me about
The oblivious man being hatless
And balding and about to get shit bombed
By the sea gull
With that liquid shit they shit
Usually two toned brown and white
Reminiscent ironically in consistency
Of some kind of antidote for diarrhoea

Therefore the daily ironies of what
Walks by your position in society
Oblivious to the roots
Of the disposition that follows
Is a frisson to the observer
In his frame of reference

He follows the bird that follows the man
Till all three are out of the picture
And that's that
Stage life left

Presupposing, it puts us in the position of,
The big stork eats the baby
Which we cheer on in our refinement
And as politically correct
But without a context
So not

Coming out of the birth canal
Is a slippery slope

And ironies abound
So work those skis
All the way to Socrates.

::

He sits watching the DVD
Has two large bowls of popcorn
In front and beside respectively

A third arm reaches into the glow
The hand takes all it can

Through the half-lit room
The hand is tempted to squeeze more
But the popcorn units promise
To pop out
So the hand learns
To ease off

Round the corner in the dim kitchen
Over the counter the hand delivers up
The salted buttered popcorn

This is rat ecstasy
Immediate and spoiled

By the leftovers left over
From the spoils all eaten

Far afield the distribution of corn
The braking parachutes
The dumpling clouds
The parliamentary representative
Chasing the *semeiosis*
Peirce on the logic of pronunciation
In the Bard
With a side of spelling
Witness in the nineteenth century
To the birth of the new
Third usage of "science"

The communal doing of it
"What in Germany they call
Logical socialism"
It effecting "the indefinite increase in
[references]."

⁘

I can lead my horse to water
This proverbial image
Will not do

I can willfully walk to the path
For thought
But there's thought dead or alive
In the will

Thought, you might say
Happens to you
Sitting in the sand whose kernels
Aquinas quit counting after a quick mulling
The ocean lapping at his feet
Wok-panned sublime with a lot of salt

How what leads to thought
And after the path that runs
Through you
How where this leads

Thoughts have signs
To coin a construction

Thoughts then have bodies
"Bodied forth" Bardied forth

Bodies that tumble
Stand down others on their heads

I'm not hard-core rational
In a "mystical shell"
I'm hard-core essence
As soft body dogged

The mechanics of the cognitive unconscious
Serve the summons
And brings you on board
The sea summed
For a horse

I lead my horse to water
He don't drink deeply
He talk deep
From the horse's mouth
Cut off in my palm
Feeling its oats

The painter without a Cary
Putting paint
Like the silk worm silk
On a sow's ear.

∷

Outside the spring snow melting
On off the roof dripping

My crystal ball
Is an onion

We carry the new freezer
Down the root cellar–like stairs
Into the basement on the farm

The big yellow Lab smoothly watches me
Descend jerkily step by step
I get shorter and shorter
Right under his nose

His soft retriever jaws
Close on my implement hat
The guys at the bottom proceed
The chef holds the lid
I like, duck
The dripping continues
Joseph and Mary are turned away
From the inn

Parmenides gets it up again
And the relocated blood
Is hard on him

He proves up
Then he proves down

My mother called back
To teach at a late age
Taught the kids some drama
How to fall
Went down like a demo-ed building
At the head and feet of the class

One of her earlier ex-students
Is too lame to get out of his truck
Jason from South Korea
Brings him out his groceries

Brings him out
You are what you eat apparently
Before you eat
That's a new one

Here's some more melt water
Such dripping
I would like at my funeral
General Intellect's hi-lo there
Standard of leaving
And desalinated tears.

⁙

I drive a jeep out of
But into
A flat relatively barren prairie
At least a little brown looking
In the early spring

Planes come out of nowhere
Strafing me, hit or miss
Is up in the air

The jeep and its line of displacement
Are a sentence left open a bit
The planes are aspects
Of an articulated world
Articulating from its side

I stop, get out, stand
And stretch, daring them
Nothing
I find some snow
Try the old yellow ink
Not in a name
But you name it

The plane with bullets like child
Puts a sign on the jeep

Not really
After I zip up the undead approach
They don't understand
What I'm doing
I see in their intelligent questions

This is the world in the making
Not as it is
Not as it ought to be
Only what it could be becoming

They leave
They seem to have stolen the jeep
The planes are finished
There are no flowers
Oh yes, I can smell them

I walk back in the later spring now
"Voltaire" in a gravelly crackly Yankee
Academy Awards voice
In my edgetable garden
Where my nephew is composting
What's left of consumed fruits and vegetables
On top of and under
Coffee grounds and egg shells

He's brought out plants
And egg cartons with sprouts
He played his guitar to in the bedroom
We've been calling the music room
But is now also the nursery

He's dug up my mother's old flower beds
Except for the tulips
Planted onions, tomatoes, cilantro
Carrots . . .
That ellipsis stands for the other seeds
And an incomplete sentence.

::

How predetermined is the colour
Of tomatoes?
All kinds of other correlations
Come to mind

When I think of red blood
The curve ball earth
Comical Polonius clouds
The resultant pink and purple evening
Just flinging out

Your neuronal distribution
Yet further distributed
We must but quit
Flung out by some correlating
Wild Spinoza

The grade two girl I would guess
In helmet on skateboard
Distributed into the movie
Before she reads the book

Therefore the pathos
Of the unnecessary shadows
Which say it all

Long side
Her own overriding Brecht
With the scene.

::

¶

The text is set in Figural, designed by Oldrich Menhart in 1940 and produced digitally by Michael Gills in 1992.

Poet, philosopher, and family farmer, CHARLES NOBLE divides his time between Banff and Nobleford, Alberta. His most recent books are *Sally O: Selected Poems and Manifesto* (Thistledown Press, 2009) and *Death Drive Through Gaia Paris* (University of Calgary Press, 2007). He won the Writers Guild of Alberta poetry award for his collection *Wormwood, Vermouth, Warphistory* (Thistledown Press, 1995).